So You Want to Vlog?

By
Andrea Valeria

So You Want to Vlog?
How to start from scratch, find your voice & share your stories

Table of Contents

Introduction

What Do You Do?

"You're a blogger?"

"Well, no, actually I'm a vlogger…with a V," I respond as I awkwardly make what they think is a peace sign. It doesn't help that with my accent, Vs and Bs sounds very similar.

After receiving some blank stares, I explain that I'm a vlogger, as in "video blogger."

Explaining what I do for a living and why I do it are everyday occurrences. That's because vlogging as a digital nomad is an occupation many people have never even heard of.

One of the reasons I got into vlogging is my love for writing, but a college professor once told me that my writing style is too conversational for literature. Ok, fair enough. But, do you know which medium is perfect for a conversational tone? Talking to the camera.

As a vlogger speaking directly and candidly to my audience, I can make jokes, convey sarcasm, or get serious when the moment calls for it. That's one of the reasons why telling stories on camera continues to excite and challenge me. On my vlog, I can express myself through my tone of voice, facial expressions, mannerisms, supporting video, and music—using the full range of communication modes to tell each story.

As I'm writing this and explaining it to you on paper, you have no idea how much I wish you could see my smirking, eye rolling, hair flipping, and eyebrow raising because that's how I fully express myself. Maybe if you've watched some of my videos, you'll actually hear my voice in your head and visualize how animated I get when I'm passionate about something—because I'm truly passionate about helping you discover your voice, promote your brand, and find your audience through this new medium.

Chapter 1

What Is a Vlog?

The word itself is a pretty recent addition to our vocabulary. Vlog, vlogger, and vlogging weren't added to the Merriam-Webster dictionary until 2009.

In fact, when I was a finalist at the 2013 Shorty Awards, the category was called Best Video Blogger. The annual Shorty Awards recognizes people and organizations producing short-form content. When I was nominated, I had been vlogging for only about six months. While I had the opportunity to attend the awards show in New York and meet some of the industry's heavy-hitters, I didn't win. But that experience made me realize I definitely want to continue pursuing vlogging. The following year was the last time they gave awards to "video bloggers." Today, the category is called Vlogger of the Year.

The Cambridge Dictionary defines a vlog as "a record of your thoughts, opinions, or experiences that you film and publish on the internet."

Before YouTube, if someone wanted to express themselves directly to the camera or share one-on-one conversations with a large audience, they would have to be a talk show host. Nowadays, literally anyone can have their own show, produce it, publish it, market it, and even monetize it.

I want to pull up another definition before we continue. I keep it quite simple, by the way (I just went to Wikipedia). Let's talk about art. We, the united people of Wikipedia, define art as "a diverse range of human activities in creating visual, auditory or performing artifacts (artworks), expressing the author's imaginative or technical skill, intended to be appreciated for their beauty or emotional power."

Visual arts (painting, sculpture, etc.), decorative arts (like architecture), performing arts, and interactive media are all listed as forms of art. Video falls under some definitions of interactive media. Do I believe vlogging should be considered an art? You better believe it!

Art is inspired by the artist's surroundings. It presents their emotions, feelings, and ideas in aesthetically pleasing or thought-provoking ways. Artists have talent and hone their skills. Most importantly, art makes people feel something. If something you see, read, or listen to awakens an emotion or inspires you to act, the artist has done their job.

A vlogger is an artist. My recording and editing equipment are my paint brushes, and my locations and on-camera delivery are my canvas.

Being a vlogger is also like being an independent musician who doesn't have to listen to record label executives. As a vlogger, I have total creative freedom. Vloggers control their content and how it's produced. We have direct access to our audience through social media. We are the Chance the Rappers of online video. He is proof that with creativity, talent, and hard work, you can do it all independently.

My favorite part about being a vlogger? I can be my uncensored self. This is something I value because when I was a TV news reporter in Tampa Bay, Florida in 2011, being myself on camera was heavily discouraged. The news is understandably meant to be serious, but it all felt too controlled and emotionless for this artist-at-heart.

The news director had me cut my hair and style it "more maturely" because I looked too young. The wardrobe department put me in pantsuits in neutral colors. My idea of creating some fun, positive stories about our community was off the table. My scripts were edited to better fit the station's concept of storytelling, and my stories were re-edited, stripped of emotion and personality.

In the television news and entertainment industry, the decision-makers might be completely out of touch, but if they think you or your ideas aren't worthy of airtime, that's the final word. This approach to video storytelling turns away so many talented on-screen personalities who have something to say. Just a decade ago, they were left without access to an audience. But in the online, infotainment world—where visual storytelling is king—your individuality, hard work, and basic equipment can prevail over industry norms and politics.

"But, anyone can do that," I've heard so many times. Sure, anyone can record a short video on their phone and post it online. But something magical happens when an undeniable talent, a charismatic personality, or a unique voice or message gets discovered online.

We've all heard the origin story behind Just Bieber, who began his career on the Internet after his mom posted his videos on YouTube. Today's decision-makers are the masses who click, like, follow, comment, and share. In the vlogging world, viewers decide what they like and want to consume more of. Yes, there's more competition out there—but passion, practice, and a quality product are still the keys to success.

Being an online content creator also leads to a more devoted fan base. In the case of Bieber, the girls who were around to see his early videos when they had only 500 views are probably now the presidents of his fan clubs. As a new vlogger, your viewers will watch you and your technique evolve in front of their eyes, and they'll become more invested in you as an artist over time. Witnessing growth creates a bond.

Chapter 2

Is Vlogging for You?

Here's another typical conversation for me:

"I also want to be a digital nomad. What do you do for work?"

After I tell them I'm a vlogger, they say, "Maybe I could start a vlog, too. What camera do you use?"

That's like asking Beyoncé what microphone she uses because you want to start singing. Not that I think I'm the Beyoncé of the vlogging world, but one can dream, right?

Don't get me wrong. I could start singing tomorrow, and you can start vlogging today. What I'm saying is that Beyoncé—like most successful artists—began with a passion and some serious talent, worked her bootylicious behind off spending decades perfecting her craft, then became the star we know.

It is not about her mic. And it's not about my camera.

How Did I Become a Vlogger?

Let's go back to 2012. At the time, watching American Idol was my hobby. Tweeting about Grammy performances was fun for me. All I wanted to talk about was pop culture and celebrities. One day, I was talking to my boyfriend at the time about Ryan Seacrest for the 918th

7

time. He said, "Why don't you start a YouTube channel about your pop culture stuff, since you like talking about it so much?"

Shortly thereafter, my "it's a Pop O.D." channel was born. Now you're totally going to look up those videos, and they're all pretty ridiculous. Oh well! That vlog was my creative outlet while I was in school getting a master's in entertainment business.

Not only was my passion project a great way to disconnect from studying, but it kept me entertained while challenging me creatively. The more I did it, the more I fell in love with the rush of coming up with an idea, seeing it come to life, and posting it for everyone to see. And by everyone, I mean all 100 people who viewed my early vlogs.

But within six months, I was being considered for that video blogging award, so…

Would You Make a Good Vlogger?

To help you figure out if this vlogging thing could work for you, ask yourself these questions:

- Do I have a passion that's potentially vloggable?
- Am I able to come up with related story ideas and topics?
- Do I like writing stories and sharing them with others?
- Do I have a point of view that is entertaining, informative, or inspiring—or all three?
- Could I ever get tired of this topic?
- Do I feel comfortable in front of a camera (or could I ever get to that point)?
- Do I have a good eye for photography/videography?
- Do I enjoy editing videos? Or, am I good at learning new software?

- Do I have the patience to spend long hours in front of a computer?
- Do I know about digital content marketing or social media?
- Will I feel comfortable with pressing that publish button?

Keep in mind that if you answered "no" to some of these questions, we live in a time when it's easy to become self-taught. Google, YouTube tutorials, ebooks, webinars…the learning opportunities are endless.

Do You Have What It Takes?

Let's say your friend Danny, who is funny and doesn't take himself too seriously, posted some great vlogs about him making salads in mason jars while wearing nothing but an apron. Sorry for objectifying your friend Danny.

Those vlogs got great reception, and it really pushed his salad restaurant to the next level. So, now you're considering forcing yourself into becoming a vlogger because you want to replicate that success for your food truck.

But, wait. Do you have Danny's charisma? Do you have a cool or unique concept? Can you publish new content consistently? And most importantly, will you enjoy doing it?

Vlogging isn't for everyone. It's time consuming. Editing can be frustrating. You will lose footage of a moment impossible to replicate. Getting the audio right is still daunting to me. People will judge you. But, the great thing about this kind of performance art, as opposed to stand-up comedy, for example, is that you don't see your audience while they're watching you. So, if a joke doesn't land and they don't laugh, you'll never know!

If you think vlogging is definitely right for you, I don't want you to overthink it. I want you to go for it. Why? Because to this day, uploading my first video blog has been the single most career-changing move I've ever made.

Chapter 3

Different Types of Vlogs

To some people, a vlog is when you turn the camera on and just start talking. Some claim a vlog entails logging your day, week, an event, or your travels in video form. To me, all the videos I've been making in the past year are vlogs, and they're all quite different from one another. So, let's skip the debate of what truly is a vlog, because you can make it whatever you want it to be. However, there is no doubt that there are different types—just like there are dance styles, music genres, and cuisines.

If you're wondering which of type of vlog you should create, here's a quick description of each of those. While figuring it out, think about what you know how to do, what topics you'd like to tackle, or what you'd like to showcase.

The Talking Head

This type of online video content was the first to ever be considered a vlog.

You set up the camera, hit record, and run off with your topic. A Talking Head vlog is usually not edited, and can be uploaded to the web just as it was shot. A Facebook Live video in which a person addresses the camera for 10 minutes can also be a type of Talking Head vlog.

I admire any vlogger who solely produces this type of vlog. If you can keep someone interested just by talking to a camera with zero embellishments or supporting videos, it's a testament to your charisma and talent. The Talking Head vlogger and their on-camera presence take center stage, supported only by their topic and eloquence.

While this type of vlogger may not write a single script, it is important for Talking Heads to tackle topics they're clearly passionate and knowledgeable about. As long as you're good at improvising and painting a picture, this is a vlog totally suitable for any topic. Whether your goal is to educate, inform, entertain, motivate, or help, you can get your point across if you're a good storyteller.

At the same time, there's also a risk of your Talking Head vlog coming across as a rant. Let's take Kanye West. He's passionate about being one of the most influential artists of his time. When he talks about this on camera, you can see that what starts as a series of logical ideas soon turns into a full-blown rant.

If you're too fired up about a subject and jump in front of a camera to talk about it, your ideas may stop stringing together with ease.

Because I'm not Kanye and don't have his size audience, if I try to deliver my stories like he does, my vlog probably wouldn't be successful. If you're trying to find your audience and connect with them, you want them to relate to you.

A perfect candidate for a Talking Head vlog is that person who everyone loves to listen to. A person who can tell beautiful stories and has a way with words. Have you heard of the vlogger Jason Silva? He's the type of on-camera personality who can undoubtedly pull off this style of vlog.

Talking Head vlogs don't require a lot of videography knowledge and skills, like shooting and editing. However, just because this is the simplest type of vlog to produce, doesn't mean that a successful Talking Head vlogger is any less talented.

Think about a rustic, farm-to-table restaurant where the food is presented without additives and gastronomic flourishes. There's an organic feel to this product. As the consumer, you focus more on the ingredients. When consuming Talking Head videos, you focus more on the creator, their talent, and their topic. It's raw and unscripted, and oh so good for you, if done right!

At the same time, this is also the kind of vlog that can easily become the most boring. How many people in the world are you willing to watch as they talk nonstop for 10 minutes on your phone? And we're not talking about Face Timing with your mom.

Recapping Events

Think of these as daily vlogs. Recap vlogs showcase someone documenting their life, from what they had for breakfast to their workouts and what time they went to sleep.

This type of content can easily become boring if your days aren't exciting. If you're going to become a daily vlogger, ensure that you're either really good at editing and can make anything seem interesting (totally possible) or that your days are totally worth watching.

Gary Vaynerchuk's Daily Vee vlogs are an example of someone whose day-to-day life translates beautifully into a daily recap of events. He and his team "document, not create" (his words, not mine) content and upload it to both YouTube and Facebook.

For people who are famous or already have a following, a daily vlog is easier to market because people are already invested in them. For us regular humans, having a successful daily vlog requires more than just documenting your life. For example, you would need to do something that's going to be cool to see every day. This is why a lot of travel vloggers opt for daily vlogs. Generally speaking, any day traveling can be presented in a rather interesting manner. On the other hand, if you spend most of your days going to an office or retail job then making dinner at home, coming up with compelling daily content is going to be a challenge.

Having a type of vlog like this go viral is also quite an impressive task. Because these vlogs are usually on the longer side—and online viewers have notoriously short attention spans—it's not easy to reach a broad audience with videos that aren't bite-sized. Something really amazing would have to happen for your Recap of Events video to jump out to viewers. And let's be honest, how often do really amazing things happen when you're hanging out at home?

Recap of Events vlogs are usually edited to tell a story in chronological order, but you can get away with having no defined beginning, middle, and end. These videos don't necessarily have to be informative or motivational, but they must be entertaining or compelling. If reality shows were distributed online instead of on TV, they would fall under this category.

Whether you're creating a daily vlog, a weekly vlog, or a travel vlog, recapping a series of events requires editing. For that reason, it can be quite daunting to edit a video every day. Think of all the footage you would end up with after a whole day or trip. For a Recap of Events vlog, all of those clips need to be condensed down to the highlights.

In contrast with the Talking Head-style vlog, Recap vlogs don't need pre-production. You don't need a script. You don't need a concept beforehand. You can just grab your camera and make sure you have enough battery to last you through the day. If you're attending an event for a highlight vlog, all you need is your ticket to the event. If you're making a vlog of your travels, just carry on with your normal travel plans and document as you go.

If you don't like to plan, voila! This might be the type of vlog that best suits your personality. Although, I will share some vlog preparation tips in another chapter that you can apply to this type of vlog.

I've made a few Recap vlogs in the past, and to me, these are the easiest ones to create. I don't have to think of what to say or worry about locations to shoot. I just followed the action, hoping to run into interesting interactions and situations. But when shooting like this, you need to ensure you're quick to catch all the important moments.

Another example of online videos that are considered Recap of Events vlogs are the Jay Alvarrez productions. You might see this guy and think, "wow, he is living the life!" This vlogger is a surfer guy pictured with hot girlfriends who spends a lot of time doing extreme sports in the world's most beautiful beach destinations. He doesn't talk in his videos. His productions are a collection of clips including lots of drone footage with stunning photography. They're edited to the beat of high-energy music.

If you also have a great eye for photography, spend time in gorgeous locations, and are great at editing, a Recap vlog could be your style.

While these types of videos require editing, it can be simple or complicated. Most of them don't even require pre-production, which lessens your workload. Recap vlogs can be a good starting point to get your feet wet in this medium, get familiar with your equipment, and practice editing.

Produced Packages

Because I came from the world of TV news, let's use it as an example of this format. A news package often starts with a "stand-up" in which the reporter addresses the camera and gives an intro of what the story will be about. These packages include interviews, supporting video, and a story with a beginning, middle, and end.

All of my "it's a Travel O.D." vlogs fall under this category. I enjoy producing these the most because I like to tell a story that is informative but still entertaining. Having a script or guests/interviewees allows me to inform my audience, while the supporting footage helps each vlog become easy and entertaining to watch.

My favorite vlogger who creates Produced Packages is Nas Daily. Not only is he a storytelling genius, he's also the epitome of consistency.

To create successful Produced Package vlogs, you must prepare beforehand. You need a concept or idea. Once you have the topic, do your research to ensure that all the information you want to present is accurate. If you're making an opinion-based vlog, your talking points should be logically ordered and presented in an attractive manner.

When you want to feature other people on your vlog, make sure you are really familiar with what they do. That way you can write a script that showcases them in their best light. I try to avoid giving them too much information in advance because I want them to have natural answers. Don't give them a chance to overthink it or get nervous.

For these types of vlogs, you also need to plan the location where you'll shoot the standups, the interviews, and the supporting footage needed to illustrate the idea. Produced Packages can take as little as two hours to shoot, or they can take a few days if you need to get lots of different footage of various activities.

This type of vlog is probably not the right place for newbie vloggers to start. It can be overwhelming to come up with a concept, write it, get enough footage, organize all the clips, and edit it in a way that tells a cohesive and compelling story.

This type of vlog may be right for you if you have previous videography experience. Produced Packages are also a good choice if you enjoy being in front of the camera but don't want to start talking without a plan. If you'd like to feature other people or make mini-documentary vlogs, Produced Packages are a great fit.

What Type of Vlog Is For You?

If you're a **Talking Head** vlogger and what you're talking about isn't entertaining, you will lose viewers in a split second. Some people who are fabulous storytellers have the power to make any topic fun to listen to. If this is you, then Talking Head vlogging will be a piece of cake. If you want to vlog about gardening but can't come up with one topic that makes gardening *sound* exciting, you either want to pick a different type of vlog or a different topic.

However, not everyone wants to elicit happiness and laughter with their vlogs; not everyone is a comedian. Some people want to educate their audience with useful tips or teach them how to do things via tutorials. These types of vlogs can spread like wildfire if you're sharing really valuable information. The key to success with this format of the Talking Head vlog is they must be entertaining, informative, or inspiring.

Let's say you're making a **Recap of Events** vlog about beer festivals. If you can manage to make this video informative by telling people when to go to these festivals, what to wear, how to get tickets in advance, what to expect, how to find the best ones, etc., you might create a vlog worth watching.

On the other hand, if your forte is beautiful photography, you have a drone, and you're a master at editing, then you could create a spectacular short video with music. This format of the Recap vlog would capture beer festivals in a way that makes people think, "I need to go to that fest next year!" Destination Recap vlogs, which also bank on their visual and musical appeal, can get the same kind of reaction from your viewers.

Or, let's admit it—you're one of the most entertaining humans in the world. It's fun to watch your day to day activities. Then, the chronological, daily Recap of Events vlog might be for you.

Finally, there's the **Produced Packages**. Just like the other two types of vlogs, these need to be either entertaining, informative, or very visually pleasing. While Produced Packages may also require more planning and editing than some other forms of vlogs, the payoff is a professional looking, tightly packaged product that may get your vlog the attention you're after. It's working for me!

Whatever vlog type, format, and style you go for, choose what best showcases your passion for and knowledge about your topic.

Chapter 4

What's Your Vlog About?

"Who will want to hear me talk about bacon?" Umm, lots of people, actually. But, you should know that your passion, delivery, and storytelling are actually more important than your topic. Plus, how many vlogs are there about bacon? I have no idea. I didn't check. The point is that it's a lot easier to attract an audience when you have a specific topic and concept than when you're trying to appeal to everyone.

There are two ways someone decides what they want to vlog about.

Aspiring Vlogger #1 is Marie. She likes to talk to cameras. She has even had some practice editing videos at her previous job. Not only does Marie know she's good at telling stories, but she's certain she wants to start vlogging…about something. She just has no idea what exactly she should vlog about.

Aspiring Vlogger #2 is Joey. He's an expert at jumping rope and teaches a fitness class called "Rope-Jumping Madness" at a local gym. He started a blog with posts like "Which Rope to Buy," "Jumping Rope for Beginners," "10-Minute Cardio: All You Need is a Jump Rope."

Do you think Joey will have an issue finding out what he wants to vlog about? Do you already know what your passion project should focus on?

Let's say your topic is clear. You're going to vlog about the fitness lifestyle. Creating videos about workouts, active wear, and healthy recipes makes sense. If you were to include some vlogs about travel and some about makeup—two of your other interests—you'll lose your audience. You might have a loyal following who loves you for the health and fitness inspiration you bring into their lives every day. If 30% of your posts start featuring photos from your trip to Europe and #traveltips, they might unfollow. That follower might be a person who likes going from the office to their home and has a fear of flying. Do they want to see their favorite fitness vlogger on a plane headed to places they have no interest in visiting? Nope. Just like that, you've turned them off. They're gone, and there's probably no way to get them to come back.

Or, maybe you're more like Marie and aren't totally clear on your topic or niche.

You might be thinking "I like to paint, I'm a mom, I have some killer recipes, I have fabulous recommendations on where to eat around Chicago, and I play the guitar. Since my vlog is going to be about me, it will feature vlogs on all of those topics."

When people say their vlog is about a little bit of everything, I try really hard to not look confused. Most "finding your niche" experts say that if you try to appeal to everyone, you're appealing to no one. You might think that doing a little bit of everything will give you more opportunities to attract a bigger audience. But, you don't want an audience of people with unrelated interests. You want a community of followers who care about the same things you do and feel united by this shared interest.

Pick a Topic and Become an Expert

When your vlog becomes successful enough, many of your viewers will consider you an expert on that subject. You might start getting approached by clients who think you're an influencer in your given field. But, if you cover a little bit of everything, are you really going to be considered an expert on anything?

Before you have a huge following, what's the best way to sell your vlogging as a service? Offer them your expertise and influence over a specific niche. On top of that, sell them your talent. Clients find it very appealing when you can produce a vlog with a creative angle that helps them provide value to their potential customers (who happen to be your biggest fans).

Let's say you have a vlog that shares home-cleaning tips. Each of your weekly vlogs is getting 10K views, a lot of comments, and great overall engagement. Your viewers are asking you questions about the best cleaning techniques, tips, and products. Now you're considering reaching out to a potential collaborator to pitch them your services. How about approaching an online store that sells cleaning supplies and products for wood? You could create a sponsored vlog post on "How to Clean Wood Cabinets." You're the perfect vlogger to do this because you're considered an expert on cleaning, and your audience trusts you on this topic. Would the same client want to work with you if your vlog talks about "a little bit about everything"? Probably not, unless you had 300K views per vlog.

Now let's say you're like Marie. I hope you didn't forget about our girl Marie; she's Aspiring Vlogger #1 who doesn't know what to vlog about. Even though you're trying to define your topic and niche, your goal shouldn't be to vlog about what others aren't doing. Don't bother aiming to find a void in the market that you could fill.

A lot of people assume that picking a topic no one else is doing will make you instantly excel. Instead, you end up with a vlog about "Endless Ways to Cook Bacon in Strangers' Kitchens." Are you going to be the only one vlogging about this? Probably. Does this mean you're going to automatically dominate that market? Well, no.

First of all, that subject doesn't have a market and for good reason. Secondly, you can dominate a market when you're talented and passionate about the subject, not because you're the only one who thought of it.

The key here is to focus on your interests and talents instead of doing way too much research in hopes of coming up with something that's never been done before. You need to love your vlog topic, to live and breathe it. You must enjoy talking about it.

Now think about a topic you have in mind, and ask yourself the following questions:

- Is this a topic you know a lot about?
- When your friends think of this topic, do they instantly think of you?
- Do you find yourself giving advice on this topic?
- Could you talk about it for hours?
- When you procrastinate, do you find yourself doing something related to this topic?
- Would you consider it one of your hobbies?
- Is it fun for you?
- Do you consider yourself an expert on this topic?
- Can make this topic entertaining, informative, inspiring, very visually pleasing, or all of the above?

If you answered yes to five or more of these questions, then you may have figured out your vlog topic. If you answered yes to less than five of these questions, your vlog is already at risk of becoming more of a pain than a passion.

If you end up picking a subject you don't live for:

- You may run out of angles to cover.
- By vlog #11, you might not look as passionate and excited about it, and the viewers will pick up on that.
- Instead of becoming a fun side-hustle or passion project, your vlog will feel like work.
- You won't find time for it.
- People will not view you as an expert, so you will have no credibility.
- Since it's not fun for you, it won't be entertaining for those watching either.
- You will end up abandoning it.

Please don't overthink your topic so much that it becomes an excuse for not starting your vlog. The worst scenario is that after one year of vlogging, you start thinking this niche wasn't the best choice. If this happens, stop and start over. You can think of that first one as your trial-run that enabled you to practice and learn what you like, what worked, and what didn't resonate with your viewers. Your next vlog will be even better.

In 2012, I was obsessed with talking about celebrities and TV shows, so that's what my first vlog was about. Did I make the wrong choice because now I'm doing something different? Nope. That was the right choice at that time. I just evolved and graduated to a different kind of vlog.

Let me refer to the career of Miley Cyrus (because I still love the whole pop culture world). Miley has gone from Hannah Montana to the twerking "We Can't Stop" phase to creating more mature, country-influenced music. If she can grow to reinvent herself, her music, and her style from album to album, you can change your vlog niche later on, too. Do what feels right at the present moment so you can start learning from the experience and developing your skills as a vlogger.

Chapter 5

What's in a Name(brand)?

It's important to really love your vlog name. You're basically having a kid here. You're going to be stuck with it forever (well, maybe not forever), and you're going to say its name over and over and over again. So, if you like it and are proud of it, you'll feel more comfortable bringing it up in conversation.

Your vlog's name will be one of the first things people see. It's essentially your business's name. Once you pick one, it's hard to change it unless you totally start over. Changing your vlog name is not just a quick rebrand or changing your logo, so think about this one carefully.

In the digital world, people start thinking of you by your username or vlog name. So, if you'd be embarrassed to be the "gardeningincutedresses" girl, then you might want to look at another name that makes you proud to share.

What if you want to use your own real name? Well, you can, of course. Do whatever you think is best for your project. If you are the star and each vlog revolves solely around you, I guess that's a good idea. However, as you're trying to make your vlog known, recognize that no one knows who you are. I'm not sure anyone would like, follow, or subscribe to the Andrea Valeria vlog. It can be beneficial and easier to achieve your goals if the viewer can have an idea of what your vlog is about by just looking at its name.

Names to Avoid

What about a super controversial name? You might turn people on or off before they even watch anything you published. You could lose viewers forever. A brand might not want to partner with you if they don't see themselves aligning yourself with your name. However, you might want to stand out and have no problem defending the name of your vlog. If you're able to stand by it and deal with the trolls and haters, go for it. Don't say I didn't warn you, though.

You also want your vlog name to stand the test of time. Now, we're not talking 10 years down the road, because in multimedia years, that's a century. What I'm talking about is avoiding trends that will no longer be relevant once you're on your third vlog. "Covfefe with Maria"? That word had its 15 seconds of fame. Google "covfefe" if you missed it. Just don't fall for fleeting trends and buzzwords when picking your vlog name.

Also, stay away from copyrighted names. You don't want to be eight vlogs deep and receive a Cease and Desist letter. Even if the company/brand that has the same name as your vlog is not a vlog itself, you could be forced to drop your name. Don't neglect to Google your name ideas first to see what you're up against.

Avoid vlog names that are too specific because they tend to limit future opportunities and collaborations. Let's say your vlog is about bacon. (I'm not encouraging drinking while reading, but if you take a shot every time I mention bacon, you'll be drunk by the end of this book.) You might be thinking, "I have to get creative and be really specific about my vlog name." So, you narrow down names, and bam! You've decided to name your vlog "The Best Affordable Restaurants With Dishes Containing Bacon" and start your journey as a vlogger. Eight months later, you're getting a few opportunities here and there. You're going to small restaurants in the area and getting quite a few views. But, you've also lost many opportunities due to this name. What if you come across a chef who's created some unique and affordable bacon dishes but doesn't have a restaurant? His work doesn't fit within the confines of your very specific vlog name.

Or, imagine that the best restaurant in all of Manhattan starts serving the ultimate, most indulgent bacon dish. They invite the best food bloggers, vloggers, and influencers to generate content for this new menu item. They want to invite you because they like your content and your voice. You email back and forth with their marketing team, and one day you get an email from this fancy NYC restaurant. Subject: Thank You!

You're excited. You open up the email, and there it is: "We really like your vlog, but we've decided we can't collaborate with you because our high-end restaurant is definitely not considered 'affordable.' Wishing you the best!"

In an effort to be specific and unique with your vlog name, you inadvertently prevented yourself from working with the heavy-hitters of bacon dining.

Because your vlog name will be with you for a while, leave room for it to grow with you. Consider how this name may need to scale up or expand out in the future. Think big, and avoid placing restrictions on your vlog name unless you're 100% you'd like to commit to that limitation. (Plus, that fictitious bacon vlog name is waaay too long. Don't do that with your vlog name, either).

Let's Pick a Name Now

I like lists. You like lists. Let's make another one that could help you name that vlog of yours already!

Before you go all in with any name you have in mind, find out:

- Can people tell what your vlog is about by just reading this name?
- Does it contain at least one keyword of your vlog topics, themes, or niche?
- Is this domain name available?
- What about the same username on Instagram, Facebook, YouTube, Twitter, etc.?
  If your vlog is called "Gardening in Cute Dresses," don't settle for garden_cute_dress on Instagram because your real name isn't available. If your name is the same everywhere, it makes it a lot easier for people to find you.
- Is anyone doing the same exact same thing or with the same name?
  If so, you definitely need to change your name, switch up your vlog type/format, or find a way to differentiate your style or perspective from that of the other vlogger.
- Might a brand/company look at this name and be discouraged to work with you?
- Will you be proud to say the name of your vlog at a networking event?
- Could you regret choosing this name a few years down the line?
- Is it pronounceable and easy to spell and type?
- Is it original enough to stand out?
- Does it make people want to click it?
- Will your target audience be compelled to know more?

As you start gathering ideas, looking up words in a thesaurus, and brainstorming with your most creative friends, acknowledge that this is an exciting part of the process. You're naming your kid here! You might not want to call it something as simple as John Smith, but you also don't want to give your kid a hard time for the rest of its life by giving it a confusing name, either. Yes, I constantly refer to my vlogs as kids. I don't compare them to one another, and I love them all equally.

Once you start making videos, you may make some bad ones. But it's not the end of the world. If six months after you start your vlog, your first videos no longer align with your brand or you look at them and cringe, you can just delete them. You can have them no longer appear anywhere on your platforms, and new viewers or potential clients will never know about those early attempts. But this is not the case with your vlog name. That's why you want to be sure you won't regret having chosen it.

Branding and Online Presence

Before you ever publish your first vlog, ensure you have the branding all done. You don't want to start with an improvised look and feel that you will change later. This is not the time to procrastinate. You need to have your online aesthetic down before you launch.

Think of this as a business. Even if your goal is to be vlogging strictly for fun, you want to stand out. Actually, I'm assuming that if you're reading this, you may want to get really serious about vlogging and maybe even monetize it down the road. Having a strong brand that doesn't look like you're putting out random amateur videos will help you get noticed.

Your Logo

What do you need to look like a pro? You need a logo!

Go to Pinterest and create some boards with logo inspirations. If you have a friend who is a graphic designer or social media strategist, hire them for a consultation and start seeing your options based on your inspiration logos.

Decide how much or how little you will use this logo. You can have it as your profile picture (although I think your face is a more personable option). You might use your logo as a small "lower third" in the corner of all your videos. Use your logo in your professional email signatures. Feature it on business cards. Having your logo everywhere will make you appear more legit, so don't publish your first vlog post without it.

Animations

For the sake of cohesiveness, all of your vlog videos must have the same visual/graphic cue.

I recommend getting an animation for your vlog. Mine has my logo, but there are many different ways to do it. I use this same animation somewhere close to the beginning of each video and a longer version of it at the very end of each video.

If you're not sure what kind of animation you'd like to use or how you'd like to incorporate it into your videos, check out other vloggers to see what they use. Whatever you decide, make it short. If your videos are three minutes long, no one will be entertained by a 15-second animation at the beginning of each one. Don't make viewers click out before they even have the chance to watch your content.

For anyone who thinks that making a logo or animation is going to be a challenge, don't stress. I can hear some excuses floating around already.

If you're thinking of making vlogs, you're probably either tech savvy or you have a computer with access to the Internet. If you think you can't create what you want by yourself, maybe you have a friend who creates motion graphics you can pay for their services. There are websites that enable you to hire graphic designers and animators on the cheap. You can get a logo for $10 to $150. Same with the animation. If you can't afford that, get creative. There are free online resources. Cool? Let's move on.

Where to House Your Vlog

You're ready to buy a house, but you haven't chosen the neighborhood. The ideal location for me might not work for your lifestyle, and vice versa. If you need the space, you might even buy two houses in different neighborhoods. But, this decision might leave you without enough money, time, and energy to maintain them the way you'd like.

The two most welcoming neighborhoods for vloggers are YouTube and Facebook. I'm going to warn you that I'm completely biased. However, I've used both, so I'll try to be somewhat objective (wish me luck) because they both have their benefits depending on what you're trying to achieve.

YouTube

Last time I checked, YouTube was considered the second-largest search engine in the world. You know the first one: Google. This search-friendly quality may work to your advantage as a vlogger, depending on your subject matter.

Let's say that you will be producing vlogs about your daily life routine and you are just starting out as a vlogger. Are lots of people actively searching for your videos? Probably not.

What if you're making tutorial vlogs with titles like "How to Use Your Phone's Newest Feature"? In this case, being on YouTube might be a great choice for you because people are searching for that kind of video.

If your vlogs are the type of content people search for, you could become a YouTuber.

Facebook

Searchable content can also become successful on Facebook. Remember that content is king, so when your content is good, your fans will find it.

One of Facebook's great benefits is that everything posted to the site—whether it's a text, image, or video—is shareable. If you're making inspirational and motivational vlogs, your videos are likely to get shared a ton on Facebook.

This doesn't happen as easily on YouTube, which means that you might lose some opportunity to be discovered if you're only on there.

Know Your Audience

Of course your choice of platform should consider your target audience. Not only their gender, age, and location, but also their behaviors. Are they spending their time scrolling through Facebook? Or like my younger teenage brother, are they busy subscribing to their favorite YouTubers?

One of the reasons why I'm on Facebook is because the people who watch my vlogs the most are women around my age. I know how my friends and I spend our time online. We are part of Facebook groups to interact with like-minded people. We want to see what everyone wore to that wedding we couldn't attend. We take work breaks by going on Facebook to see a few heartwarming videos. My friends share vlogs that inspire them and content that they think their Facebook friends would appreciate. Since I feel like my vlogs could inspire a woman around my age to get out of her comfort zone and travel more, I post my vlogs exclusively on Facebook.

You've used both of these platforms, so you know what they're capable of and how we use them.

What Matters to You?

What motivates you to start a vlog? Are you seeking video views or do you aim to create an engaged community? This is one of the most important distinguishing factors between Facebook and YouTube.

On YouTube, if viewers only want to watch videos, like, and comment on them, they can create an anonymous account like beachgirl2918. On the other hand, Facebook members have a profile that typically showcases their personal and/or work life through photos. I'm not saying it's impossible to create an anonymous user profile on Zuckerberg's platform, but it's certainly not as common as on YouTube.

Facebook is a social media platform where people go to connect with each other, while YouTube is a video-sharing website/app. If your goal is to connect with your viewers, engage with new followers, and build a community that can trust you, you might want to focus on Facebook.

Because of these user differences, the comment section on a given video may read very differently based on the platform. Let's say Susy McBrown is a mom of two toddlers. She is an active user on both Facebook and YouTube. On Facebook, she shares pictures of her kids at the park, and her coworkers like her photos. She also has a YouTube channel. It's the same one she's had since she was in college: susylikestheboozey. We all make dumb decisions when we're 19.

After Susy watches my new vlog on Facebook, she might comment "Where in Belize did you stay?" If she watched the same vlog on YouTube, and she thought my dress was too revealing, she might post "Cover up, b****!" in the comments because no one knows who susylikestheboozey is.

So, imagine that you're a new vlogger (or even if you've been doing it for a while), and you're excited because you got a comment on YouTube. Yep, I still get excited about every comment. But, instead of a fun question, an interesting perspective, or some basic support for your work, you now have to deal with trolls who hide behind a fairly anonymous user profile.

My old pop culture vlog was YouTube only, and I received some harsh comments on there. Someone asked if my face hurts from all the gestures I make. Kinda funny, but also hurtful. That commenter didn't have a profile picture, of course.

My current vlog, "it's a Travel O.D.," is on Facebook, where I have yet to see a bully in my comment section. Interesting conversations do happen on there and sometimes there's controversy or members of my little travel-loving community respectfully disagree. But, Facebook has turned out to be a great space to receive honest comments, suggestions, and even ideas for future vlog topics—for me.

Both of these platforms has tons of unique features. If I were to continue to compare Facebook and YouTube, this chapter would consume the majority of this book. Plus, I have already given away my opinions on the matter. I can only speak from my vlogging experience. You have to do your own research to determine which platform is best for your vlog. Good luck picking where you want to live!

Oh, wait, we can't wrap up this chapter up without a list, amirite? Here's a few things to remember about vlogging on YouTube and Facebook:

- Care about building a community? Facebook!
- Are your topics going to be searchable (like how-to videos)? YouTube!
- Would you rather be more shareable? Facebook!
- Longer content? YouTube!
- Are you making vlogs to sell your services? Facebook! (Because it's connected to your page where you can have a services section)
- Do you know what type of content works on each one? You must do some homework!
- Most importantly, do you know where your target audience spends the most time?

Are there other options to host your video content? Sure. There's Vimeo, for example. However, I'm not even going into that for the purposes of vlogging because you want people to easily find your content.

Chapter 6

Getting Started

"But, what if I run out of topics to vlog about?"

If you're experiencing self-doubt or hesitation, rest assured that we all experience this when jumping into a new project. However, if you are legitimately terrified that you won't be able to come up with ideas for your vlogs, let's stop and think and go back to chapter 4. That's the chapter about defining your concept and asking yourself questions to ensure you're picking the right niche for your vlog.

The truth is if you pick a subject you are truly passionate about, you'll never run out of things to vlog about. Think of someone in your life who is obsessed with a specific sport. Do they ever stop talking about it and their favorite team, the games coming up, the new recruit, etc.? That's your goal. Find something that you love to talk about with your friends, a topic that comes up all the time, and vlog about that.

Generating Ideas

Let's get to how you can actually come up with some topics for that vlog of yours.

I have a friend who we will call Mely. She makes vlogs about food and recipes. We were talking about our vlogs, and she told me she needs to have her brainstorming session of the week in order to come up with a topic. I thought she was working on some sort of unique project and had to meet with her team to brainstorm. Nope. Mely has brainstorming sessions every week by herself. She sits down and comes up with ideas for her next vlog.

Me: How long is each of your brainstorming sessions?
Mely: About 2 hours. Sometimes longer, sometimes shorter.
Me: WHAT? Don't you already have a running list of ideas?
Mely: No—wait—what do you mean?

First of all, I was shocked. I assumed that every vlogger, content creator and artist has a list of ideas to refer to. Once I shared with Mely my trick to always having topic ideas handy, her life changed forever (and yours will, too).

I call my brainstorming method the Grocery List approach. When I was growing up, my mom always had a piece of paper on the fridge. If we ran out of anything in the kitchen, we wrote it down on this list. Then, when it was time to go grocery shopping, my mom would take this list with her. Easy, right? Imagine if, instead of doing this, my mom sat down to think of what we needed before every trip to the grocery store. Aside from being a complete waste of time, she'd probably forget things. This is what my vlogger friend Mely was doing: wasting precious creative time and missing out on a bunch of ideas that came to her during the week.

To use my Grocery List method, you don't even need to carry around a piece of paper because you can easily create a list on your smartphone. Mine is called "Vlog Topic Ideas" and features a video camera emoji, in case you're curious. You should see the amount of unused ideas that live there. When I read some of those, I'm like "hmm… not sure what I was thinking," but that is perfectly fine. It's better to have too many ideas than not enough. Some of these evolve into better concepts, but if the ideas weren't on the list to begin with, that wouldn't even happen.

Where Do Ideas Come From?

Articles/Blogs/Other Vlogs

An article on a cooking magazine about quick lunch ideas helped Mely realize it would be a great idea to vlog about "3 Lunch Recipes That Don't Need Refrigeration." What ideas could you generate from your online browsing?

Comments on Blogs/Vlogs/Facebook Groups/Instagram Posts

Your vlog is going to be about a topic you love, so you'll probably be consuming a lot of relevant information. If you are going to be uploading vlogs teaching people how to do workouts at home, you probably follow some fit girls on Instagram who do just that. Pay attention to what people are commenting. If you see multiple comments or discussions on a Facebook group about where to store your gym equipment in a small apartment, well that's a potential vlog topic right there. Now, add it to your Grocery List before you forget!

Chatting with Friends

I was talking to a friend from back home who told me, "The other day I was with Manuel and he joked that you must have a sugar daddy because you travel so much." Ummm… no I don't, Manuel. But thanks for the vlog topic idea!

Once you get your vlog started, your friends will probably have some questions. If those questions are vloggable, write them down. Rule of thumb: If people constantly come to you asking for advice about a certain topic, you might start noticing some recurring or interesting questions. Add all of these ideas to your Grocery List. Maybe one of them can become a stand-alone vlog or string them all together for an FAQ vlog.

Immersing Yourself in Inspiring Places

If you vlog about dancing and you haven't hung out in a dance studio for a while, chances are you're missing out on opportunities to get inspired. Talk to other dancers. Go to dance classes and seminars. Attend a small dance production. Get out of your comfort zone to learn hula dancing. Check out that salsa club. Make a point to watch a city's ballet. Surround yourself with what inspires you and vlog ideas will come to you.

Meeting New Friends in the Field

Since I created my travel vlog, I've started following and have met so many travel bloggers, vloggers, and Instagrammers. I came across their accounts because we have similar interests. They inspire me because they speak my language. They have the same goals or struggles as I do. That means that every time we engage with each other online or in person, I get to add a few more potential vlog topics to my running list of ideas.

Whether you meet new friends in your field at a networking event or on Twitter, engage with them more or hang out with them, if possible. Your fellow content creators and thinkers are the best motivation and a great source of inspiration. I can see some of my online friends reading this now and thinking that I talk to them just to get vlog ideas. I don't. I promise!

Your Own Experiences

The more you do something, the more you learn about it. Let's say I have a vlog in which I talk about working remotely, but I actually work in an office. Do you think I have enough personal experience in this area to come up with ideas?

If you live the life you preach about in your vlogs, it's much easier to write and talk about what you've experienced. For example, on my vlog I share a bunch of tips on how to meet people while living as a digital nomad. Why? Because I am a digital nomad, and I can talk about all the different avenues I've used to make new friends everywhere I go.

If you vlog about cooking, cook more. Get out of your comfort zone and buy different ingredients to see what happens. Go to an Indian cuisine cooking class, and vlog about that. Take your camera with you to the farmers market and document how you pick out seasonal vegetables. In order to vlog more, you have to experience more. So go do that!

Just Listen

The videos you watch, the people you talk to, the questions you get, the comment sections online: they're all sources of ideas. Sit at a table with friends and just listen. That's how you get ideas from your everyday life.

And when the lightbulb goes off, be sure to write down your ideas! I've heard songwriters do this all the time. They're hanging out walking and read a graffiti that sparks an idea for a song lyric. They write it down. Allegedly when Taylor Swift gets ideas for song melodies, she instantly records them on her phone's voice memos. So, don't forget to add every idea for your vlog to your Grocery List.

When you write down ideas that just come to you, make your note as detailed as possible. If your friend made yummy guacamole but left it out overnight, and that inspired you to create a vlog about "What You Should Know When Cooking with Avocados," don't just write "avocados" on your list. You don't want your vlog idea list to resemble an actual Grocery List! You want to make it easy for your future self to skim the idea list and pick your next brilliant vlog topic.

I happen to get lots of ideas while talking to people. Actually, to be more accurate, by listening to them talk. Every single time, I whip out my phone and write down my latest idea on my running list. I'm pretty sure whomever I'm talking to thinks I'm rude for texting, but that's okay. I have vlogs to make.

Chapter 7

Pre-Production

When I tell people that each Produced Package video I make takes me at least 10 hours, sometimes people don't believe me. Considering my vlogs are usually about two minutes long, it's not easy to grasp how it could possibly take so long to create.

I've had more than a few interactions that go something like this:

Curious Random Human: So, why does it take you that long?

Me: From pre-production to shooting and editing…it's a long process.

Curious Random Human: Pre-Production?! But, you're shooting a vlog, not a freakin' Hollywood movie!

Let's get this cleared up: pre-production is any type of planning, strategizing, or brainstorming that happens before the cameras start rolling. Cleaning your room to shoot a "Talking Head" vlog is pre-production, just like putting together a few bullet points and writing emails to schedule an interview are part of pre-production. Pre-production can also be like what it took for Nas Daily to prepare for his vlog in which he invited hundreds of people to his home. Everything from putting out an invite on Facebook to his brother flying into the city to help out and having his mom cook for everyone is considered pre-production.

We like lists, right? Here's a list of tasks that you may complete as part of pre-production:

- Conceptualizing/brainstorming (or just deciding on a topic!)
- Writing a script (or bullet points or questions to ask)
- Finding people to be in the vlog (not always the case, of course)
- Finding a crew to help (if your vlog happens to be a bigger production)
- Scheduling (or even just finding time in your calendar)
- Location scouting (when you shoot outdoors, this is something you must do)
- Permits/planning (you might need to talk to a few people to shoot at a certain place)
- Preparing equipment (even just making sure your batteries are charged)
- Wardrobe (I've made vlogs where I've had multiple costume changes)
- Props (I had to buy lots of cereal at the dollar store one time)

So, now you know: Even the simplest kind of vlogs require some planning beforehand.

Scriptwriting

Out of all the elements in the pre-production stage, we should definitely chat a bit more about this one. Of course, some types of vlogs can be completely unscripted. For example, you're shooting a one-minute Talking Head vlog. It's part of your weekly series in which you share your forecast of the upcoming soccer game of your favorite team. You might be the most eloquent human being on Earth, you don't ramble, and you're totally clear of what you want to say. Cool. You hit record, give your thoughts on camera and you're good to go. You do not need a script.

However, sometimes a script is needed. By "script" I don't mean that you need to write a screenplay and recite it word for word (but you could). The concept of a script can be as loose as a list of runway shows you'd like to talk about when you record your Talking Head vlog about New York Fashion Week.

Or let's say you're covering the annual Beer & Bacon Festival in a Recap of Events-style vlog. So, you'll be documenting what you see and experience, and your vlog will showcase what you were able to capture on camera that day. For something like this, you might not need to write a script before you get there. You'll talk to attendees, ask them questions, try some bacon and maple cupcakes, and shoot it all while talking about your favorite beers as you taste them.

Another example is if you're shooting a vlog a la Gary Vaynerchuk's Daily Vee. D-Rock and the team follow Gary around and document his day. For this kind of shooting, a script isn't needed.

But, that doesn't mean you can always get away with talking to the camera without a game plan.

Let's return to that vlog you're going to make about the Beer & Bacon Festival (because I actually made a vlog at one of those festivals some years ago). As part of my pre-production for that video, I made a list of the breweries that would be there, along with a few facts to say about each of the flagship beers. Prepping like this is always a good idea. You want to be over-prepared with interesting tid-bits. This kind of script can work well in the middle of montages and help make your vlog more informative (as well as entertaining).

Then there's scripting the kind of vlogs I make. Produced Packages require more structure. In this example, let's say we're vlogging about a person. If you don't already know this person, you'll need to do some research to find out their most important characteristics. What's unique about them? What draws people to this person's story? You can discover really interesting facts about people by having a conversation with them, researching their background and becoming familiar with their work.

Don't Say That

When deciding what to say and ask on camera, remember that every word on screen occupies valuable space and time in your vlog. Don't waste any time stating the obvious or sharing things that aren't super interesting. Every single sentence needs to pack a punch. Great vlogs don't include fluff.

Here are a few examples of opening statements that should never be uttered, along with stronger openers to catch someone's attention:

Don't say: "This girl has a really cool life. Let me tell you why."

Try something like this instead: "Maria has lived in 28 countries and speaks seven languages to prove it."

Deliver a concise intro that's more attention-grabbing than a vague comment. In a short vlog, there's no time for general statements.

Don't say: "Look at this variety of cakes! They make them in all shapes, sizes and flavors."

Say something like this: "If you come to this bakery with an idea for a cake, they'll make it happen. No request is too crazy!"

The first statement tells viewers something that can be illustrated by showing a clip of the cakes in all shapes and sizes. Narrating the action on screen by stating the obvious doesn't add to the video.

Don't say: "This is Caye Caulker and it's the prettiest beach I've ever been to."

Instead say something like this: "It took me two flights, two boat rides, and a few mosquito bites to get here… but I'm definitely not complaining. Welcome to beautiful Caye Caulker!"

Again, saying something that the viewer can already see does not add value to your vlog. Instead, revealing a bit of what happened behind the scenes makes it relatable. You always want to make sure you're telling your viewers what their eyes can't see.

Don't say: "As you may know, this is my third day here on the island of Bocas del Toro. We're heading out to see what we can find."

Instead say something like this: "Heading out without an itinerary for the day. When you're in Bocas del Toro, sometimes it's better to just go with the flow!"

With the suggested script line, you're letting viewers know you're traveling without an itinerary. That's more interesting and specific than "heading out see what we find." Also, this could be the first vlog they see of you, so telling them it's your third day might throw them off. You never want to make your viewers feel like they've missed something and should go back to watch your earlier videos before finishing the one they stumbled upon.

Don't say: "I met this person and we clicked instantly. You might like them too!"

Try this instead: "Rafael went from having an office job to touring with a circus... Here's how he did it."

Your viewers want to know what people do, and most importantly why and how they made it happen. Sure, your personal connection with the star of your video can be interesting or funny, but this kind of vlog is not about you. This is about showcasing your subject by highlighting what might resonate with your audience. Lead with a fact that makes people want to keep watching. If the story of how you two met really is fantastic, you can mention it later.

Storytelling

Whether you're vlogging about your day, a restaurant, a workout, or a person, tell a story that will resonate with your viewers. Find a way to make your viewer feel like they want to be part of what they're seeing. If it's a vlog about a beach, you want viewers to feel like they should go there for their next vacation. If the video is about a person, you want to make viewers think, "I want to be their friend!" A good storyteller can make any situation interesting.

With great footage, you can transport people to a place. But with a great story, you can inspire them. Your story will drive your vlog. If you aim to really develop one skill over time, it should be storytelling.

Once you're set on a topic for your next vlog, begin by writing down the most important and interesting facts you know about it. If you're not sure, go do your research.

Let's say we're making a vlog about an individual. You can check out their website, read their blog posts or Instagram captions. Read the questions their community asks them because that's what people want to know! Find stories about them that explain how they've gotten to where they are, what makes them stand out among the rest, and highlight it. Do they employ a cool marketing strategy? Mention it. Did they earn an Emmy Award? Don't just talk about it; tell people something they don't know, like how many tries it took this person to finally get nominated.

Once you have enough cool facts, reorganize them so they flow from one idea to the next. Start strong. Then, in the middle, tell people how this person does what they do. To end, focus on something inspiring, something that will leave your viewers thinking or ready to take action. Always relate it back to your viewer.

"But, what if I'm making vlogs about workouts?"

Start off strong by telling people how effective your workout is, and hook them in with the uniqueness of what you have to offer. Then, explain how they can do it. Keep in mind that people don't always have the skills or equipment to perform a workout like you because you're the expert. So, get in their shoes and give them modifications or unique tips to maintain good form. Wrap up your video with some motivational messaging to inspire your viewers to check out your next workout. Leave them with a feeling of "yes, I can do this." By the way, the format of this example also applies to vlogs that feature recipes, make-up and other tutorials, unboxing and so much more.

Whether you're showcasing a person or a workout, don't make it sound intimidating or complicated. As a vlogger, you should seem like a helpful, accessible friend with something cool to share.

Here's a useful formula for structuring a Produced Package script:

BEGINNING:

- Tell your viewers that this is the best thing they've seen!

- Insert super interesting fact to illustrate how you're about to show them something unlike anything they've seen lately.

MIDDLE:

- This is why!
- Tell viewers how they, too, can do this… or how they'd feel if they were at this cool place!

END:

- Remind viewers that they can do it, too… they should try it… they should go there, too.
- Do viewers feel inspired by what you've shown them?
- Insert your call to action. Give them a trigger that would remind them of you or a prompt that would motivate them to spread your message to others.

This structure isn't ideal for every topic nor every vlogger's style, but this is a good way to organize your bullet points when you aren't sure how to get from one point to the next in a logical way.

While there aren't exactly rules to this art, when it comes to writing scripts, successful vloggers live by these basic guidelines:

- Leave out any basic/generic statements.
- Don't make it all about you, all the time.
- Remember that your audience needs to find value in what you're giving them, whether it's information, entertainment, or inspiration.
- Don't repeat your facts.
- Be sure you're highlighting characteristics that your audience will appreciate.

- Keep your script casual and conversational. Use words you'd normally say.
- Don't pretend to be good at stuff and know things outside your area of expertise. Let your on-screen guests (the real experts) do that.
- Write about what people can't see on the screen, so your script avoids stating the obvious.
- Include feelings and emotions. You're not writing a news story.
- Make it relatable.
- Add humor (if appropriate and your comedic timing is good).
- Write scripts that sound like you're talking to a friend.

Once your vlog script is ready, read it out loud a few times and time yourself. Make sure it flows and has the right tone, pacing and energy. Make adjustments if it's too long or short.

Recognize that you're going to make many videos before you start crafting your own style and voice. You can get inspired by watching other vloggers, but eventually you'll find a style that's uniquely yours. If you watch too many of my vlogs, for example, you might unconsciously pick up some of my tone and groove. That's cool and I'm flattered. But, I really want you to find your own identity in the vlog world and give us something we're not used to seeing. If someone watches your vlogs then meets you in person, they should feel like they already knew you. Sure, you may be more animated on camera, but don't fake it. Vlogging isn't an acting gig. Be upfront, be honest, and most importantly, be you.

Chapter 8

Shooting Your Vlog

Where to Shoot

Lots of vloggers have a studio in their homes. Don't get scared when you hear the word studio, though. It doesn't have to be a complicated and expensive setup. A home studio is just the location where you always shoot.

If you're an indoors vlogger, having the same backdrop in all or most of your vlogs can be a smart strategy. Your home studio could be in your living room with a colorful bookshelf in the background, a map of the world on your wall, or some Pinterest-inspired backdrop (if you're a good DIY-er).

If you don't always want to have the same background, you could go the green screen route. I used a green screen for my first vlogging setup because I'm an overachiever. If you're tech-savvy and might enjoy the heavy post-production required with this type of shooting, you may want to give this a try.

If you're shooting outdoors or on location, have a checklist of what you need while shooting. There's nothing worse than arriving to a location only to realize you forgot your memory cards.

Be Prepared

Here's my basic shooting-on-location checklist:

- Camera
- Charged Camera Batteries
- Memory Cards
- Tripod
- Microphone
- Back-up batteries (for microphone)

Feeling prepared is the secret to nailing it. Even if you're heading out to just document something as it happens, you still want to have a game plan.

If you're thinking, "I'll just get all the footage I can," you might face a few obstacles down the road. For example, you risk running out of battery when it's time to capture something important. Or, you could end up with way too much footage. "That can't be bad," you might think. But oh, it is. Every single second of footage you end up with is footage you'll have to watch again and again and again when it's time to edit. While you want a variety of clips to make your video dynamic, you don't want too much of something that you won't even use. If you got enough good shots of the models at a runway show, you can stop shooting, save your battery, save your memory cards, and save yourself some time in front of the computer.

Let's say you're going to Coachella to shoot a Recap of Events vlog. You still need to do your research.

Being prepared (at the very least) means knowing these kinds of things:

- What artists are performing and where?

- Which performances do you want to shoot? What songs are you interested in capturing? (You don't need to shoot the whole set.)
- Do you have any vlog guests to feature? (Scheduling is important. Set up a time to shoot before your guest gets sweaty, lost in the crowd, or drunk.)
- Is there footage you want that you can't get after dark? (Shoot this first!)
- Does the beer tent close at a certain time? (Shoot that before you get caught up in the performances.)

To shoot a Talking Head vlog, your preparation is different. Of course, you need to write a script or have a guide so you don't end up rambling or missing valid points.

When I did more of this kind of vlogs, I used props and outfit changes to keep it more engaging. My preparation included looking at my script to determine which props would work with the topic. I then headed over to the nearest Dollar Store to stock up on funny little items for the lifestyle/comedy vlogs I was making. I also spent time doing my hair and makeup and picking out outfits that would look different from my last few vlogs. Hey, that counts as preparation too, right?

Whatever your vlog style might be, envision your finished vlog, think of any steps you need to take during shooting to achieve that product, and prepare for it.

Memorizing and Reciting Your Script

Some of you worry that you can't learn your script. If you were to ask me to memorize the two minutes of script I prepare for each vlog, I couldn't do it either. That's why I cut up each of my scripts into small chunks, and then record each portion.

Through editing you can make it flow nicely. There's no need to stress over learning all of your lines. Vlogging is not like performing a live play. Because you don't have to worry about memorizing all of your lines, you can focus more on your delivery. You don't even need to recite your scripts word for word. You can use bullet points and ad-lib, if that works for you. If you ramble a little bit, that's fine. You can get rid of the extra lines in post-production.

Here's Your Strategy:

1. Divide your script into small paragraphs (one to five sentences each).

2. Save the script on your phone.

3. Learn one portion of the script by repeating it a few times in your head.

4. Once you have it down, start rolling the camera.

5. Before saying the lines, say "3,2,1." This makes editing more efficient because you know when to place your starting mark without missing the first word and having to go back.

6. Even if you nail the line the first time, I recommend saying it three to five times total. You never know what could have gone wrong. A gust of wind could have ruined the audio. A person in the background could have flashed their private parts. Seriously, crazy things might happen. Your hair might have been terribly out of place. By having a few shots to pick from, you can guarantee that you'll get yourself sounding your best and looking the most natural.

7. After each line, stop recording. Having everything segmented like this makes it easier when you edit. It's especially helpful when you're looking for a particular line. Looking through two minutes of footage is easier than looking through 20 minutes of nonstop video.

8. Repeat this process for each of your lines until you've made your way through the script.

Being on Camera

Random Aspiring Vlogger: Andrea, you look so comfortable in front of the camera. I'm not sure if I can do the same!

Me: Have you ever tried it?

Random Aspiring Vlogger: Not really.

First things first: Get in front of the camera and start practicing. You have a cell phone with a camera, and most computers have a webcam. Those two are good enough for you to start practicing while recording then watching the footage.

Take notes: Do you have any weird ticks you can avoid doing? Are you doing weird things with your hands? Do you look down or away from the camera when you're nervous? Those are the kinds of details you should notice when you watch yourself on camera. The next time you practice, focus on fixing them.

Sounding natural on camera is one of the biggest struggles vloggers face. It's important that you speak in a language that is normal to you. Don't say "There was a kerfuffle in my household after my spouse came forth with the incorrect perishables, or, rather the lack thereof" if that's not something you'd say on the daily. Keep it normal. "Ugh! My husband forgot to buy the groceries, and I almost wanted to kill him."

An easy way to sound approachable is if your voice, tone, and language are the ones you use in real life. The key is to appear on screen exactly as you do off camera. Sure, you can turn up the bubbly factor, the smiles, or the excitement, but it's important that you remain true to your real-life persona.

Why is authenticity important? Because viewers recognize fake. You've seen reality TV shows in which the stars' interactions look painfully staged, and you were probably turned off.

If you're loud, be loud on camera. If you're quite serious, don't try to be silly. If you're sarcastic or goofy, keep being exactly that. Don't try to be super cute and funny just because you see other vloggers doing that.

Another big mistake I see some vloggers doing? They try to emulate TV presenters and end up making robotic and unnatural hand gestures and poses. If it's not how you act in real life, it's not how you should act in your vlogs. Practice until you appear as normal, relaxed, and natural as possible.

Get Hyped

There are things I do before I shoot a vlog to get myself in the right frame of mind every time.

- I listen to music to put myself in the best possible mood. It's all about having the right energy. When people watch you, they pick up on the smallest things, so being in the right mindset can make you seem more approachable.

- This one might seem weird, but I don't eat before shooting a vlog. The vlogging adrenaline is all I need.

- I always do my hair earlier that day. Instant confidence boost!

These might seem like insignificant details to some, but to me, they're the keys to shooting footage I'm going to love. Establish your pre-vlogging routine and make it your own tradition.

Let's Shoot

Never hit the record button and shoot like a grandpa on a safari. You've seen these videos, right? They never pause, the footage is shaky, and there's a lot of footage of the ground.

The ideal way to shoot (to make it easier on yourself during editing) is to make lots of short clips. Let's say you're shooting a travel vlog of your experience in Tulum, Mexico, and you're walking along the main road. You don't need a five-minute, nonstop clip of you walking.

Most of the time, you will be shooting yourself. This is when the camera's flip screen or some camera's WiFi feature (that allows you to connect it to your phone, for example) comes in handy. Aside from ensuring that you're in focus, you also want to establish a nice frame for yourself. A shot that's too close can look awkward. However you decide to shoot, you always want to have enough headroom. Don't cut your head off, and don't set up your shot with too much sky or ceiling. Generally, you want to shoot yourself from the waist up, or do the occasional close-up shot. You can be in the middle of the frame or to the side, that's up to you. I suggest using a mix of both in a single vlog to add movement.

Sometimes, you can shoot a whole script with your shot framed the same way. But, it's cool to switch it up. For a super animated talking head vlog, try changing camera angles or locations for every single one of your lines. Let's say you're shooting on a beach. You can try a wide shot, then another shot with a high angle while you're sitting on the sand, then a regular medium shot with palm trees in the background, and so on. Shooting indoors? You can play around with a medium shot, to a close-up, to a wide shot. It all depends on your set, style, tone, and feel!

Always let your creativity fly to get unexpected shots. The beauty of vlogging (unlike shooting live videos, for example) is that you can later edit and cut out all the pieces in which you sounded or looked weird. The more you do it, the more you'll figure out what works for you. It's all about finding your unique vlogging style through trial and error.

During your shoots, you want to avoid distractions.

I'm comfortable enough to shoot my vlogs on a busy street. People even stop and watch like I'm doing some sort of performance. At this point, I'm great at tuning them out and delivering my lines. In the beginning of my vlogging career, though? I wasn't able to do that. In fact, I used my first vlogging studio in my living room only at night because that's when there weren't text messages coming in and I had zero chance of getting distracted.

I recommend that you vlog in an empty room. Put your phone on airplane mode. Make sure you're looking at the camera, and that you're not getting distracted looking at yourself in the flip screen. In fact, once you've set up the shot, you could even hide the screen so you avoid letting your eyes wander. Try to avoid wearing uncomfortable clothes or being too hot or cold. Everything needs to be just right. The more you're in the zone, the more relaxed you'll look in the video.

Oh, and ditch the chairs! Well, if your vlog is about pottery-making techniques or unboxing products, it might make sense to sit down. But, standing up gives you a more powerful posture that exudes confidence and energy. There's a reason public speakers are standing and walking across a stage while delivering their message. Can you imagine Steve Jobs presenting a new iPhone while seated?

Now, there's something I'm personally against when it comes to vlogging: prompters and cue cards. Using them affects the naturalness of your delivery. If you're not totally familiar with your script or if you're concerned about reading or following a prompter, it prevents you from being in the moment and adding your own flare. Plus, we can see that you're reading. As a vlogger, you want to have honest convos with your audience, and prompters/cue cards take away from that friendly feeling.

It's okay to practice in front of a mirror. It's okay to repeat your lines over and over until you nail it. What's not okay is being afraid of what other people might think of you. That's their problem, and they don't pay your bills!

Collabs and Shooting Interviews

Why would you shoot an interview for a vlog, you might wonder. While the most common form of vlog is a single person talking to a camera, you may want to do more and expose your vlog to a new audience.

Let's say you have a fitness vlog that features gyms. You might want to feature a gym owner/fitness instructor. Or, you could be a makeup vlogger and invite a guest to your vlog to showcase a specific makeup technique or product. This is known as doing a "collab" (or just collaborating).

A collab is a surefire way to expand your viewership by exposing your vlog to the audience of other people in your niche (your collaborators). Whether your collaborator is a gym owner or a vlogger in your field, collaborating with them will mean they will market your video because they're a part of it!

Every collab video I've made with someone has been shared by the other person through all of their social media platforms. Plus, their parents usually get really into it and share the life out of that vlog! Nothing better than having another content creator's loyal followers discover you.

My other favorite thing about doing collabs? The networking aspect.

You don't necessarily have to know these people in advance. I've met tons of people via social media and then in real life for the first time the day we go out to shoot the vlog. It's especially motivating to meet up with someone you've never seen before to work on a creative project together. Meeting and being surrounded by people with similar interests can inspire you and teach you new tricks. Bonus: You two will probably become friends. Oh, and when they have a project in the future, if you two worked together and the vlog came out well, they'll probably think of you. The perks are endless!

However, when you have guest stars, the scripting and shooting become a bit more complex. Shooting an interview is always going to be more work than shooting your usual vlogs, but should be a good return on your time/energy investment.

As much as you'd like to hear what your guest has to say, you also want to have a clear idea of what you want from them. You should have a script.

To write these scripts, first do a lot of research on the person you're going to feature. As I describe in the script-writing section of this book, I dig up a few interesting facts about my guest, which I use to tell their story in a way that fits with my vlog's theme. In the middle of the scripted stand-ups, I leave space for asking the guest some questions. These questions are important because your guest's answers are only as good as your prompts. It's in your power to ask questions that will evoke some emotion. Avoid yes or no questions, and instead ask "how you feel about…" or "what's your take on….". From these questions, you'll get the best soundbites by extracting clips from their answers.

Your goal in one of these collab/interview vlogs is to mix what you have to say with your guest's soundbites to tell a story. Don't cut these up too much or you'll risk changing your guest's message or presenting their ideas out of context.

When you're shooting with someone, ensure that they're comfortable with you. They might not be used to being in front of the camera, so make them feel at ease. The more relaxed they are, the better they'll appear on screen. Give the interviewee room to be themselves. Ask questions that will allow them to sell themselves in an honest and humble way because this will look great on your vlog. Surprise them with a question they're not expecting to get a reaction you wouldn't usually get. Include a few fun questions. You're not a hard news reporter on 60 Minutes. Don't put someone on the spot with tough questions. You want them to be the best version of themselves, and that's only possible by being friendly and genuinely wanting them to do well.

You also want your viewers who don't know your guest to think, "wow, I want to do that" or "I'd love to hang out with that guy." To accomplish this, every aspect of the shoot with this other person should be a fun because that's what comes across in the final video. Play music between takes. Dance the nerves off. Joke around with your collaborator. When someone watches a vlog with you and your guest, they should assume you're friends, even if you met them that day.

All of your interactions with your guests should be with the intention of presenting them in their best light. Your guest will appreciate that and, therefore, will be proud to share your video.

Tips for Shooting a Collab or Interview:

Details like these can take your vlogs from amateur to professional.

- Don't give your guest the questions in advance. If you do, your guest may come to the interview with prepared and rehearsed answers. This won't sound or look natural, and you won't get honest reactions from them.
- Chat with your guest before putting them in the spotlight so they can get comfortable with you.
- Assure them you will use only their best takes. It's all about trust.
- Tell them that if they mess up, it's okay because they can just start over or correct themselves and keep going.
- If they're nervous about looking at the camera, you can stand to the side of the camera (outside of their frame). Ask them to look and talk to you instead of the camera. This interview-style shooting is more newsy, but works just fine.
- Remind them to talk how they usually do. Sometimes people see a camera and feel the need to start getting fancy. Keep it super casual and conversational.
- Ask your guest to always answer in complete sentences. When you edit, you're not likely to include the part where you ask the question, so having complete sentences from your guest will help you edit their story so it makes sense.

- Feel free to shoot your stand-ups right before the interview while your guest is around. This helps because they might see you screw up and start over, so they'll know it's perfectly okay to do the same.

Aesthetics:

Once you frame the shot with your guest, ensure they look good. If they're slouched over or their underwear is showing, tell them. Tell them to fix their hair, give them a towel if they're sweaty, give them a few seconds to regroup and start over if they're too nervous. Make sure to hide the mic wiring. It looks really unprofessional to have a wire hanging over someone's shirt when it could be tucked in. You want your guest to be happy with your vlog. If their undies were showing, they might not share it or they may even ask you to take it down.

Get it Right the First Time:

Be on your game, technically speaking. A technical issue could prevent you from getting that money shot or the perfect soundbite. It will hurt. Believe me.

- Do a test.
  Watch and listen before you shoot all of the interview. Do that a few times throughout the interview. Your guest's necklace might start hitting the lavalier mic midway through the shoot.
- Make sure the memory card is in.
- Make sure the microphones are on.
  Can you imagine if you shot some great footage with a busy CEO only to get home and realize your video has no audio?
- Double-check to see that you actually hit that REC button.

B-Roll

If you're totally new to the video world, let me hit up Wikipedia to define b-roll. This is "supplemental or alternative footage intercut with the main shot." During a filmed interview, you see supporting clips over the talking head portion. That's the b-roll, and you're going to need to capture some for your interview-style vlogs.

I'm a big fan of using it to cover parts of the interview that are boring to stare at. The b-roll illustrates what the guest is talking about while giving the viewer something interesting to look at that helps them learn something beyond the guest's spoken words. B-roll can also be used to provide visuals during your own voice-over segments of the vlog.

To make dynamic videos, I recommend having an array of clips to pick from that illustrate the same scenario, person, or situation. Aim to have tons of b-roll to play around with. Get shots from different angles. Use different techniques like pans and tilts. Do close-ups, wide-shots, and medium-shots. Put your camera on a tripod, then get some hand-held clips. If someone is looking at you while you're shooting, they should think, "They're really going for it."

Let's say you have a travel vlog and while walking down a street in Tulum, you find that famous coconut ice cream cart guy. Here's what you should do to capture b-roll in a situation like this. For five minutes, go all out and get as creative as possible, getting all the shots you can think of. Ideally, you'd get the following shots in five- to 10-second clips.

- One wide-shot from the other side of the street
- A close-up shot of the man smiling

- An over-the-shoulder of you and him together (with the camera on a tripod)
- A hand-held shot of the man scooping ice cream
- A low angle of all the people waiting in line (kneel down to get this)
- One beauty shot with the lights reflecting through the trees
- A pan from the street that ends with the man interacting with a customer
- A selfie shot of the man giving you the ice cream
- A close-up of yourself eating the ice cream (with the camera on the tripod)
- An extreme long shot of the man walking away

See? One man and his ice cream cart in 10 different clips.

While shooting b-roll, think about your editing process and the final outcome. Don't go crazy like a parent at a dance recital shooting the whole darn show. You don't want to end up with a boring, five-minute shot of which you can actually use only 20 seconds. Instead, you want to shoot one minute of dynamic footage. This means you'll have less video to go through while editing, and almost everything will be usable. That's how you get lots of visually-pleasing clips that are not shaky, random, or boring. You can then edit them into a montage with music or use them to cover a talking head.

In many cases, this approach to shooting b-roll is better than shooting an uninterrupted, five-minute interaction. But, here's two instances in which this approach wouldn't work:

Let's say you're shooting a guitar player and you want to use the player's music in the scene as the track of your video. In this case, don't stop recording to shoot from another angle. You can still move around and get a variety of shots, but don't pause and hit REC again.

Just keep going. That way, the music won't be chopped up when you want to use it as background music.

Or, if you're shooting a speaker, a conversation, or an interview, you don't want to have random, cut-up pieces of their words. This might cause your final vlog to misconstrue their message.

Tips for Shooting B-Roll:

Avoid shaky footage at all costs. Whether you're using a tripod, your arm, or a selfie stick, don't make your audience dizzy. Remember *The Blair Witch Project*? You want to avoid that style. A lot of vloggers get footage while walking. This is cool as long as you can figure out a way to do handheld and keep the camera steady. If your vlogs are going to be adventure-oriented, you might even want to invest in a stabilizer. There are accessories that can help you achieve stabilization while being in motion.

Don't go crazy with camera movements. Physically moving around will undoubtedly give your videos more energy, but crazy camera movements might be off-putting. Avoid panning and tilting too fast or abruptly. If you can get closer, do that instead of zooming in to preserve video quality. Your goal is to capture smooth shots. Otherwise, you'll be disappointed as you're looking through your footage and notice that so many shots are unusable.

Chapter 9

Editing

If you've never edited a video in your life, I'll be honest. This is when some of the most exciting moments happen.

The editing process involves reviewing your footage and piecing clips together to tell an engaging story. A good editor can make a boring event look exciting and a low-key person look larger than life. However, editing is also when some of the most frustrating moments arise. Editing tragedies will happen. A computer will crash and you'll lose all the work you've put in for the last five hours. Or, you just won't be sure how to make all the clips flow together. You should also know that editing is very time consuming!

I sincerely hope you aren't thinking that you can read this chapter to become a video editing expert. Even after 10 years of editing video and five years of using the same program, there is no way I could know every single technique and feature it has to offer. In fact, I probably learn a new one every time I edit. It's about practice and having the patience to play around with the software. In my case, I took a few video production classes. I've also benefited from online tutorials. Most importantly, I've spent thousands of hours editing and crafting my own workflow. As a vlogger, it's your responsibility to put in the time to learn how to edit effectively and efficiently.

Here's a couple life-saving tricks:

My closets and drawers might be a mess, but my editing workspace is always flawlessly organized. It helps me move quicker, and will probably help you, too.

Don't delete your original clips from your memory cards until your vlog is ready and uploaded. Be extra cautious with what you delete and when you format your cards. Few things are more heartbreaking (as a vlogger and editor) than losing footage forever.

The Editing Process:

- Unload all of your footage onto your editing software.
- Watch all of your clips. If you shot three hours of footage, you will have to watch three hours of footage to make your selections.
- Group the clips into categories. I usually do script, interview, and b-roll.
- Make one folder/bin for each category and drag the pertinent clips into each folder.
- Create one video-editing timeline or sequence for each category. This is how I organize clips and start putting them together.

Selecting Clips:

I start by looking through my own talking head clips in which I'm delivering the script or the spoken content that I ad-libbed. I find it easier to drop into my timeline only the material that I will potentially use. So, if I did 10 takes of my script, I select the best ones and put them all in my timeline back to back. I do the same thing with each line.

If I'm editing a vlog that includes an interview, I do the same thing with my guest's answers. I watch everything and pick the best full sentences spoken by my guest. These are the interview sound-bites. I extract these portions and place them in my sequence.

When you do this part of the process, choose clips in which your guest is saying something really great. If they messed up or rambled, keep going or momentarily save that clip to see if it can be salvaged somehow. Here you will end up with longer clips (than the ones of yourself) because they were responding to your questions (instead of delivering scripted lines).

Now you can move on to selecting b-roll. This part is easy! If you followed my recommendations, you will have lots of short clips. From each one, extract the best five seconds (give or take). Drag them to your timeline.

Maybe you're wondering how long the editing process typically takes me from the very beginning until I've reached this stage. It all depends on the type of project and the content. If I'm editing one of my Talking Head vlogs, which are two to three minutes long, this part of the editing process probably takes me one hour. If I'm editing a full Produced Package vlog that contains interviews and b-roll (also two to three minutes long in total), I've probably put in about three hours of work, going through footage and selecting my favorite clips. I like to take it slow when editing, so take these numbers as a vague estimate that you could ultimately shatter if you find a quicker strategy.

At this point in the editing process, you have sequences full of clips that you could potentially use. If you're doing a Talking Head vlog, you'll have one sequence. Whereas, you'll have three or more sequences if you're making a Recap of Events or Produced Package vlog.

If you're a hoarder in real life, try not to be a hoarder in the editing world or you'll end up with absurdly long vlogs. You have to be really objective. Does this clip help tell the story or is it composed so beautifully that I must keep it? If not, get rid of it instantly. It gets a little bit complicated when picking your best line out of five good enough takes. Eliminate like a champ until you end up with the winner.

This gets harder when going through your interviewee's best soundbites. Not only do you want to pick their best statements, but they should sound comfortable and natural. A lot of us say "ummm" when we talk. But, if your guest gave you a killer one-liner but they did a long "ummm" in the middle, you can still use it. But, good friends (and great editors) would delete that "ummm."

Make conscious decisions when picking clips. While you might have found an interesting soundbite, it needs to also fit your vlog's theme. If your vlog is about how your guest makes the burgers served from their food truck, you want to stick to that story. The guest might have told you a great anecdote about how their kid eats only cupcakes that look like burgers, and you cracked up. But, if it doesn't directly add value to your story, you probably don't want to include it. Maybe you can save this clip to use it later for a compilation vlog of the best bloopers. Or, just email the clip to your guest so he can forward it to his wife and laugh about it during dinner time. Sometimes, I save clips like this with the laugh included to use it as a teaser to the vlog on another platform. Or, you can try using a laugh like this (without the anecdote) at the end of your vlog to humanize your guest and make them appear more charming.

Once you have your best takes, the best soundbites, and your selection of b-roll, it's time to start arranging your official timeline! Woo hoo! This part of the editing process is usually quite exciting because this is when you get to start crafting the story.

If it's a basic Talking Head vlog, you put all your best takes together and off you go. If you're making one of the other two styles of vlogs, this is when you can play around with your content. You can put your lines together with a soundbite that was the perfect continuation to your statement.

Let's say you talked about Radiohead performing at Coachella, and you have clips of Radiohead's performance. Put those two together. You can leave spaces between all the clips where you are speaking to make montages to music, too.

Or, you can grab the b-roll of each burger to use over the talking head clip (covering it).

Another thing I do is take any moments when I'm not smiling, I'm doing something weird, or my hair or lighting doesn't look good, and I cover those shots with b-roll.

I can't possibly suggest all the options you have at this stage in the editing process. This is when your creativity should take over. Try a hundred different things until you find a storyline that makes you proud. You're not just creating an ordered sequence of clips here. Showcase your talents as a storyteller and entertain, inform, and inspire!

Chapter 10

Fine-Tuning Your Vlog

Just when you think you're done with your vlog, there's more to think about before you can export your video file, upload it, and publish. Post-production is intense, I tell you. Let's go down a list of other important details to consider.

Music

You could totally upload a vlog without any music whatsoever. I've personally never done this, though. While it's absolutely a matter of style, I think that any vlog could benefit from having a music track in the background. Whatever your topic, find music that fits well with your story and vibe.

As much as you might like a particular Jay-Z song, you shouldn't use it or any other copyrighted song! Both YouTube and Facebook identify when you're using a song you don't have the rights to. They usually kill your audio or take the video down altogether. You might have heard that if your work is a parody, your variation of the song is considered fair use. Well, I got my Justin Bieber "Sorry" Parody video taken down after it had 15,000 views. So, save yourself a headache and never ever use music that you don't own or have the permission to use. Recently, Facebook has been teaming up with music companies to find alternatives, so always research your platforms to see what options are out there for you.

The good news is that the need for music is another opportunity for you to collaborate with other creators. You can actually search for music producers, beat-makers, and musicians who will make a beat or instrumental song just for you. I've seen a lot of this type of connection-building and resource-sharing on social media. You could also search on YouTube and music-focused platforms like SoundCloud, and message the artist there. Or just hit up cousin Mikey if he can make some dope beats.

If you don't feel like networking to find music, or you need a very specific type of track, you can also search online. Let me make this Google search really easy for you: type "royalty-free music." You'll get tons of websites that offer music downloads you can use for the background of your videos. "Royalty-free" doesn't mean it's free. Rather, it's a type of licensing that allows you to purchase a song that's not copyrighted, so you can use it forever for different purposes. However, there are a bunch of websites that do offer these songs free of charge.

Audio Levels

Audio editing is often overlooked by new editors, but bad sound can turn off your viewers in a second. Having a good microphone is the stepping stone to good sound quality, but it doesn't not end there. Audio is actually the technical aspect of video editing I battle with the most. It's easy to mess it up, but you should always make the sound of your vlogs a priority.

Let's say you have edited your video and selected a background track. This track has one volume, your voice has another volume, the b-roll is all chopped up (which makes the volume go up and down abruptly), and your interviewee speaks very loudly. All of those differences in sounds might make for a very uncomfortable listening experience. Imagine your poor viewer is watching your vlog while wearing headphones and bam! A clip with an over-modulated audio almost ruptures their eardrum.

To avoid this and other audio issues, you should always revise your audio levels. A video should never be published before ensuring that the audio levels are uniform without ever hitting the red (which would indicate it's uncomfortably loud). You can view and correct your audios as you go or after you've edited the whole vlog. I find it easier to do it all at once at the very end.

Normalizing audios can get very advanced, but as long as you get these basics straight, you'll be okay.

- Adjust all of your vlog's volumes. Do this clip by clip, keeping them all in a safe zone in the green and generally under 0 decibels.
- Check out your b-roll audio. Most of the time, you want the sound of b-roll either really low or muted.
- If your music is paired with voice, keep it low enough so that it doesn't compete with your speech or that of your guest.
- When the music is playing by itself, you can bring the volume up.
- Don't forget to correct the audio of sound effects, too.

Color Correction

Small details really make a difference.

During the production stage, ensure that your footage has good lighting. In post-production, you can go one step further to really make all your images pop. This is when you should fix all colors that look off or unnatural.

Fixing the color of your videos is as easy as dropping "auto color" filters or effects on each of your clips. However, you should learn more about white balance, temperature, tint, saturation, and highlights/shadows. These are good starting points for basic color correction, which can be performed with the built-in features of most editing software. While professional color correction can get relatively complex, you might not need to go that in-depth when you're just getting started as a video editor.

Captions

Picture yourself in a doctor's waiting room. While you wait, you scroll through Facebook. Videos autoplay and you start watching them. Have you noticed how many videos you watch without even turning on the sound? People watch videos on mute while someone's sleeping next to them, while they're on the bus or in an office. We're able to do this because most contemporary videos have text, titles, or captions.

If you've seen a Nas Daily video (if you haven't yet, what are you waiting for?), you'll notice that he always includes his signature white and yellow text transcribing every single word said in the video. It's simple. Videos without text don't get as many views. I don't have an actual statistic or source for this claim, but I know it's true because I skip right over videos I can't watch without unmuting, and you probably do it, too.

Every editing software has a feature to create titles. It's sort of a tedious (long) process, but I really encourage you to do it. One of the big advantages of including captions is that they're big enough to read on smaller devices. It's perfect for all those people who watch on their phones.

However, if you just do not want text in your video file, that's cool, too. There's another way to do it. Have you seen the closed captions on Facebook and YouTube? As a viewer, there's an option to turn those on or off. These transcripts can even be auto-generated. Both YouTube and Facebook have this feature. While you do have to ensure that all of the words were picked up correctly by the caption generator (especially if you're like me and have an accent), this feature can save you a ton of time.

The best part about having captions? You're not excluding members of the audience who are deaf or hard of hearing. Accessibility readers will pick up on the closed captions and make it possible for these viewers to enjoy your content. Captions also help viewers who aren't native speakers.

Graphics

Another component of a professional-looking vlog is graphics or animations.

Your art can be as simple as a transparent file of your logo used at the end of each vlog or more complex, like an animated intro or outro. Some people go for the logo on a corner throughout the whole video. It's a matter of preference, but these are the details that will elevate your vlog's overall production value.

If you go for an animation, make it very short. I learned this the hard way. On my very first YouTube channel, every single one of my videos had an intro of me dancing around and making funny faces. This intro was a whooping 15 seconds long. I think I used that on my first dozen videos. I soon realized this was a terrible mistake when I checked out my video insights and stats and saw that a lot of people were getting annoyed and were either fast-forwarding to skip the intro or straight up exiting out. I was losing viewers. (I've made mistakes so you don't have to.) So, animations (whether they are intros, transitions, bumpers or outros) are a great addition to your blog, but don't make them long or boring. For ideas, research what other vloggers do in respect to their graphics.

You can get fancy and go beyond your editing program. There is specialized software designed to create motion graphics and visual effects. If you have time and the willingness to learn, you can create magical imagery to go along with each and every one your vlogs. Is it necessary, though? No. Don't get overwhelmed thinking you have to do it all. Less is more, and getting started is your priority.

Chapter 11

Equipment

Imagine you go to an Italian restaurant and order lasagna. As you're savoring each bite, you think this is the best lasagna you've ever had. Minutes later, none other than the chef himself stops by your table and asks about your meal. You respond: "It was amazing. What oven do you use?"

The equipment—whether it's an oven, a camera, or a paintbrush—is only a tool that allows you to produce the art you share with the world. Without ingredients like talent, creativity, good storytelling, strong production value, and practice, a vlog will not be engaging, even if you have the latest camera model and the newest drone on the market.

Now, this does not mean you're going to grab a Motorola Razr (shoutout to anyone who got this reference) and start vlogging. One of the main differences between an amateur-looking vlog and one that seems legit is the production value.

Most of the time you can't achieve super high-quality lighting or audio with zero equipment. So, if you want your video to look extra sharp, you might need to make an investment.

But, I want to bring up a conversation I've had about 50 times in the past year:

Me: You said you wanted to vlog. When are you starting?

X Human: I can't start vlogging yet because I'm saving up for the best camera on the market, a microphone, and light kit.

Me: When is that going to be?

X Human: I need to sell my car first, wait for my tax return, and I'm hoping to get a raise. As soon as that happens, then for sure I'll start vlogging.

Me: So, like 1 year?

X Human: Yeah, maybe...

If you're reading this book, you might not have started your vlog yet. But, if you're putting off your vlog for a reason like the one above, let me stop you right there. This is the perfect moment to drop a quote I heard through someone I was featuring in a vlog. My vlog guest quoted the founder of LinkedIn, Reid Hoffman, who once said: "If you are not embarrassed by the first version of your product, you've launched too late." Of course, if you have the opportunity to avoid embarrassment, do it. However, the later you start making your vlog, the longer it will take you to reach your goals.

What You Should Buy

My friends of "Nowhere Men" publish videos on Facebook that reach 1,000,000 views, and they shoot with an iPhone. No joke. At the same time, I know people with professional digital cinema cameras that produce content a lot of us wouldn't want to watch for more than a couple seconds.

So, this is a decision you have to make on your own. Do you want to spend $5,000 on equipment before ever publishing your first vlog?

Or would you rather get started with what you have or can afford to buy now? The latter means you can finish this book and start brainstorming about your first vlog!

Here are some things you should consider before buying more equipment than you need.

If your vlogs are going to be destination travel vlogs that feature scenery and landscapes, you might need a drone but you might not need a lighting kit. However, if you're shooting recipe/cooking videos, you probably need a lighting kit, and you for sure don't need a drone. You might also need a specific kind of tripod with an arm that can fully extend to get shots that resemble a flat lay.

That's why your equipment needs depend on your approach and goals as a vlogger.

Sorry, I can't tell you which specific brands, types, or camera models to purchase. I know you might have been expecting some help in that department, but it's just not fair for me to make assumptions about what could work for you. Every vlogger has a different setup that works for them.

Here's what you should consider before you drop coin, though.

- Will you be shooting indoors or outdoors? This could determine if you need lights and what type of microphone.
- Will you have a helper or will you be a one-man-band? You can't carry around a camera, tripod, drone, underwater camera, and selfie stick all by yourself. However, with a team, you could manage.

- Will you be moving around or are you always going to shoot in one place? If you're going to have a vlogging set, then you might want to buy a backdrop.
- Is it going to be just you on camera? This can also help determine the type of microphone you should buy.

Don't Bother Buying This

Don't try to get all the best equipment at the beginning. Start small. You can always upgrade later.

When I started vlogging, I created a little studio area in my living room. I wanted to shoot every vlog in the same place, but wanted the freedom to change backgrounds. I ended up buying a green screen backdrop (about $30 online) and stuck it to my wall. Since I had no idea how to operate a green screen, I spent days and nights learning from online video tutorials. Was this necessary? No.

Because I was using a green screen, I also needed studio lights, which are 100% necessary if you want to do chroma keying (the technique used to replace green screens with another background). Trying to impose a background on a green screen without the proper lighting is an impossible task. I once posted a very geeky Facebook status that said something like "Doing a poor job lighting a green screen and expecting it to work is like doing a poor job as a parent and expecting successful kids."

So, I bought a lighting kit for about $150. The price for my camera and lens was under $700. The first microphone I purchased was a clip-on lavalier (it wasn't even wireless), and it cost me around $30. Finally, I got a tripod (which I still use) for about $20. In total, I spent about $1K on my first vlogging set. You could spend much less or easily spend much more.

How to Make Your Equipment Choices

First of all, the audio should always be a priority to you. If you're talking on camera and there's background sounds overpowering your voice, that's an easy way to turn off your viewers.

Make sure your camera has a microphone input. Which microphone you end up choosing is secondary (or you can even own more than one). I tested so many microphones before I learned which one works best for me. If you buy a camera without an input for an external mic, you might later watch your poor-sounding videos and realize how important it would have been to have this capability.

Another thing that comes in handy when shooting your vlogs is having the ability to see yourself while you are setting up your shot. If you are always going to have a camera-man at your disposal, this isn't necessary. But, if you're like most vloggers, you're going to be a one-man-band, so you need a camera with a flip screen or with wifi capabilities to connect to your smartphone.

These little flip out screens make it possible for you to frame yourself, make sure you're in focus, and check your hair and makeup. If this appeals to you, make sure you can turn the screen all the way around; not all cameras have that capability. I have shot 90% of my vlogs entirely by myself. So, without this feature (and a tripod), I would not have been able to do so. Flip-out screens or the wifi feature: a must. Case closed.

Unless you are diving into the world of live videos in which your viewer sees all your raw footage, you'll need editing software. An edited piece always looks more professional and, in the end, will attract more viewers. Some people use very basic and free editing software, and that might be all you really need. However, as you get more and more advanced as a vlogger, you might feel the need to upgrade your editing program. My very first videos were edited with the default program that came on a lot of computers in 2004. I used a different one in college and another one while I was a TV news reporter until I finally found the one that works best for me.

As with your camera, it doesn't matter which editing software you end up using. All cameras gather footage. All editing programs allow you to piece together your footage. It's a matter of preference and figuring which one has the features and capabilities you need. So, do your research.

Here's a checklist to take with you to the store. Just kidding. Who goes to stores anymore? You can buy these online:

- Camera (with microphone input and flip screen)
- Extra camera battery
- Support (tripod, Gorillapod, selfie stick, mount, etc.)
- Microphone
- Lighting (if you're shooting indoors)
- Computer
- Editing software
- Memory cards
- External hard-drive

Whatever equipment you end up with, it's in your best interest to study it. Get to know your camera. What can it do? Does it have any features that will make your life easier? Does the autofocus make loud sounds that are going to interfere when you're recording? Do you know how to use white-balance? Sit down with your new vlogging kit and the manuals for each item and have a serious study session. As you learn, do a bunch of test shoots and get really comfortable with everything. And have fun getting to know and love your new best friends!

Chapter 12

Final Words of Advice

If you had the chance to pick the brains of the world's top 100 vloggers, you'd probably learn hundreds of different editing styles, processes, tips, and tricks. You'd encounter many different suggestions when it comes to which equipment to use. You'd hear why some vloggers prefer one editing software over another and why some publish on only one platform. Most importantly, you'd find that successful vloggers are motivated by a variety of goals.

The reason I vlog is probably not the same reason you're motivated to try it. Becoming a vlogger has given me purpose and the ability to express myself. Having a hobby I love completes me.

Whether your goal is to vlog for fun, promote your business, increase your online presence, establish a personal brand, market your skills, or as a creative outlet like journaling—you should take on the challenge. If you're creative by nature but haven't discovered how to share what you have to offer, vlogging might be it.

Now, let's dive into the professional aspect of being a vlogger.

I want you to know that it is possible to make a living out of vlogging, even without 5 million likes on Facebook or a million YouTube subscribers. Remember that views on a video-sharing website is not the only way to monetize your content. You can sell your vlog services to companies, partner with brands, or receive payment for including product placement in your vlog.

Your portfolio of vlogs gives you leverage, so put out quality content and do it consistently. Nowadays, that's an admirable talent and a highly marketable service.

I've had many professional opportunities stem from my vlogging experience. In the past five years, I've met inspiring people through my vlog. I've joined secret Facebook groups for creators. Some viewers came across one of my vlogs and hired me to make videos for their products (this is without me even reaching out to them). Thanks to vlogging, I've been invited to travel on all-expense paid trips in different counties. For me, someone who loves to overdose in travel, those opportunities are a big deal.

I mention this because the same thing can happen to you. If you want your niche to be about "successful creative entrepreneurs," your vlogs will help you meet them. If your goal is to market your health food store, a viewer may become your next client. By expanding your skillset, connecting you with people who share your interests, and giving your message a bigger audience, vlogging can help you get closer to your dreams.

That said, I've had a few regrets in my vlogging career.

Some mistakes actually turn into lessons. Like that one time I wore really bright pink lipstick as a joke, and it turned into my most popular vlog ever. (I now keep my makeup more understated.) Then, there's the lost footage. The times when I forgot to hit the record button and missed a money shot. The vlog that could have been stellar, but I gave it a dumb title that didn't quite capture its essence. The two-year hiatus when I took a corporate job and completely forgot about vlogging. After that, I had to restart from scratch: new vlog, new topics, new name, new channel, starting a community back up from nothing. In hindsight, it was a great opportunity to evolve and rebrand. I actually appreciate all of my losses because I probably won't make those mistakes again.

What's the one true regret I have when it comes to vlogging? I didn't start earlier in my life. I don't see the many vlogs I've made with under 300 views as a failure. A vlog that I published and tanked makes me prouder than the week when I could have produced a vlog but didn't.

You have to start somewhere. Even though my first vlog's topic is borderline embarrassing to me now, it's still up there on the web. It's a reminder of my progress, and I'll forever be proud of that day I decided to publish my first vlog. Putting yourself out there is not easy. However, I see vlog #1 and remember the first of those adrenaline rushes that happen when you share a vlog. The elation when the Internet is about to watch the story you have to tell. I hate waking up early—except when I schedule a vlog to autopublish at 8:00 AM. That's how exciting it continues to be years later.

Let me tell you about the day I realized it was time to leave my excuses at the door and get started as a vlogger. It was back in 2012. I was sitting on my living room floor in my apartment in Orlando, Florida while eating seaweed salad. Oh, I had furniture, but I just really enjoy carpeted floors. I knew I could make some fun vlogs and I had lots of ideas. However, I also enjoyed mindless downtime like watching DVR'd episodes of reality TV competitions. Making a weekly vlog would take up all my free time, I thought. Plus, I was a former TV news reporter, but now I would be posting funny vlogs? Seemed like an odd career trajectory. I didn't know what people would say or think.

For ridiculous reasons like those, I was doubting every step of my decision. If you're reading this and you're experiencing similar feelings, you can relate to what I'm talking about—even though it sounds dramatic.

That day, I opened Pinterest and a red graphic with some white text caught my attention. The quote said: "A year from now you may wish you had started today" by author Karen Lamb. I never thought I believed in signs. But, as I said some expletives to myself, I acknowledged how true this quote is and how much I had been slacking. That same night, I went online and bought all my vlogging equipment. Maybe I acted five years later than I should have, but it's never too late.

I don't want you to wait for one more excuse to dissuade you from starting your own vlog. You purchased this book and got this far. But, maybe you're still waiting for some sort of validation.

So, you want to vlog? Go do it. This is your sign.

THANK YOU

To my mom, Pilar – literally nothing would have been possible without her.

To my brother, Juan Diego who truly doesn't care about this because he's a teenager.

To my friends – always proud of me when I create cool things.

*

To my book editor, Dana Kantrowitz who I found thanks to a Facebook comment, and has become the person that will forever help me make sense in written form. (She didn't edit this, so she might hate the wording. Sorry!)

To Kalilah Hayward & Claire Merle – my very first readers. These two were the brave ones to read this when it was still really messy and not all jokes were landing.

To Rob Zawadski who gave me the idea for this – my first book.

To everyone I ever texted for title or subtitle feedback.

*

To my beyond-amazing 'it's a Travel O.D.' community who say I inspire them to do what they love or travel more. In reality, you all inspire me to create more stuff you will enjoy watching and reading.

*

Finally, to everyone who has ever watched any of my vlogs. You are more than just a view count or a like. You're my online family!

39409441R00053

Made in the USA
San Bernardino, CA
19 June 2019